# your sun will rise again

jess norris

ISBN: 978-1-7382272-0-4

*for the inner child in all of us*

who shied away from showing their true selves and finally found their voice.

the first time I put my thoughts into notes, I was lonely and felt completely engulfed by everything I was feeling. I didn't know that anyone else could possibly understand what I was feeling. when I started posting my writing on tumblr and found other people who related, I was *shocked*. my posts were gaining traction, and I finally didn't feel so alone. this book has been a long time coming. a lot of the poems go back to 2016, my first year in college. it's in three sections to represent the journey I have been on. it only felt right to make my first section all the sad stuff since that's how this all came to be, but I promise it will get lighter with time.

I hope you enjoy my journey and stick through to see the light.

## contents

into the darkness

I don't think there's anything more painful
Than knowing you have so much love and passion inside
of you,
But not knowing how to pour it out into those around
you.

Sinking.
Slowly but surely,
Until I've reached the bottom again.
The nights become longer
And my mind becomes foggier.
The only thoughts that consume my brain
Are those that push me closer to the edge
Every single day.
I'm fragile.
I'm weak again.
The bottom is approaching faster than ever this time
And I don't know how to help myself back up
Before I'm swallowed by the darkness below.
I grasp at the tools I've been given before,
But not even those are capable
Of hoisting me out of the hole
I've found myself lost in.
I don't think I can help myself this time.
I let myself suffocate.
I've sunk.

My insanity and temper got the best of me and
I'm laying in bed wondering how I ruined the one thing I
cared about most.
It always amazes me how such a gentle person can turn
into a complete storm;
Destroying those around,
Shattering the ones they care about,
Demolishing relationships.
It's like a switch is turned on inside me
And within a matter of seconds I'm a completely different
person.
I hate who I am,
I want to be better.
I'm trying to be better.

      *- self sabotage tendencies.*

Ripped from the hands of their mothers,
The ones who should have showed them love
And strength,
Teach them culture
To pass down through generations.
But instead they were stolen from their homes
In hopes to turn them into something they're not.
A genocide that left nothing but pain and hurt in its wake.
The anguish and damage
Leaked down the generations,
Stealing lives and culture.
The babies stolen from their communities
Never shown love,
Never shown safety,
Never shown comfort.
All they knew was pain.
How could a human who was never nurtured
Nurture their babies in return?
How *dare* you say their trauma doesn't affect us.
A leaky faucet will never be fixed without the proper care,
It will continue to leak and leak and leak
Until someone steps in.
That someone is me.
And from here on out,
I promise to start the healing
That my ancestors never got to start.
      - *their pain is ours.*

I hate you.
I know this is petty
But I don't know what else to say to you other than
*I hate you.*
I can't begin to explain the bitterness that overtakes me
Every time your name is mentioned
The frustration that fills me up
Every time I think of all the things you promised me.
So much of my writing was dedicated to you.
You seem to have a talent of taking things that were once beautiful
And turning them into a dark angry red,
Including myself.
I want to stop missing you.
I have to stop missing you.
This is the last thing I'll ever write for you.

There is so much pain in my heart
For the little version of me
Who hid themselves away,
Diminishing themselves to nothing.
Confined to the moulds
Because all they had ever been told
Was that their mere existence was nothing but a sin.
The little version of me
Who became everything they're not
To please those around
But only grew to hate themselves instead.

They tell me to let go
Of my hyper vigilance tendencies,
But how do I do that
While still honouring
The little child inside me
Who once used those tactics
As protection.

As a kid I thought growing up fast
And being mature
Was something everyone was meant to do.
*And so I did it.*
I became the peacekeeper,
The reliable,
The good one,
The one always there at the drop of a hat,
The therapist,
The parentified child.
I wish so badly I let myself be a kid,
I wish so badly I could go back in time,
Hold little me in my arms
And tell them to play their little heart out.
Do the kid things,
And worry about kid stuff.
Why was I more concerned about my parent's financial
state,
Or if my brother took his meds,
When I should have been worried about homework and
after school parties.
I'm teaching myself how to be a kid again
At 25 years old
And as freeing and fun as it sounds,
I'm grieving the childhood
I never got to experience.

I feel the confused stares,
Double takes,
The awkward tension when someone doesn't know how to
address me.
I hear the way those words meant to harm me
Roll out of their mouths so effortlessly.
I see the looks on their faces when they walk into the
bathroom and see me washing my hands,
I make a point to say something quickly
So they can acknowledge that it's where I'm supposed to
be.
I see the way they look at us as I walk down the street
holding my girlfriend's hand,
I feel the sadness in my chest when my dad doesn't call my
girlfriend
My *girlfriend.*
And yet every day despite it all,
I still choose to live authentically
And freely.
Even if it means at the discomfort of others.

I was doing better.
It's been a couple months since the last time I felt so
alone.
But once again,
Slowly but surely,
I started falling back into my old habits.
I got stuck in routine,
And I spent all my free time alone in the darkness of my
room listening to sad music,
Doing anything to drown out the sadness in my head.
It came out of nowhere and surrounded me completely,
I couldn't escape the black ash I was covered in.
It rooted itself into my heart
And all I could feel was the heaviness in my chest.
No matter how hard I tried,
I couldn't help but let it consume me.
I want to be happy.
I can't do this anymore.
Someone tell me how to be free,
*How to breathe.*

I want to die,
Yet my biggest fear since I was a kid was death.
I want to love so deeply,
Yet I can't seem to let anyone in long enough because
I'm terrified of being loved.
Isn't it funny
How you're scared of the things you want most?
   - *contradicting myself.*

I haven't been myself lately
And one of my biggest fears
Is not losing those around me,
But losing myself entirely.
I've always been scared I would inherit
The same anger and rage as my father,
Or the worrying and anxieties of my mother.
I'm afraid that one day I'll wake up and not be myself
anymore.
I've noticed myself snapping at the littlest things
And getting so in my head when someone's tone changes
towards me.
Without even noticing,
My biggest fear has already come true.
I already see myself turning into everything I was once
scared of.
I can't keep doing this,
I need to find myself again.

I want to shout your name from the rooftops
In hopes that you'll hear me and come back home.
We're all here,
Waiting for you,
Can't you hear us?
You left a hole in our hearts when you left
And I think we'll spend the rest of our lives
Trying to make it whole again.

I've begun to lose myself
In pieces of the hopeless love I've immersed myself in,
Losing who I am in an attempt
To become who they would want.
Becoming someone else,
Someone who is not me.
I drowned myself in alcohol
And filled my lungs with the toxic smoke of cigarettes,
Doing anything to fill the void
That is left
Of who I once was.

I remember sitting in the pews
Surrounded by my classmates,
Listening to the priest
Preach about
The perfect families of Christ,
But only the ones with a
Mom and a dad.
How many of them
Are like me?
How many of them
Wish they were "normal?"
We sing the church hymns,
My favourite -
Children of the Light.
I can't help but ask myself,
Can I really be a child of light,
If I have so much darkness
And supposed sins
Inside me?

I can't help but think about
All the times I didn't say
I love you back
Because I was too embarrassed
To show you my love.
Because saying I love you
Meant showing you the real me.
So instead, I turtled away,
Put up a wall and
Shied away from your hugs and kisses.
Those big warm hugs that I ache for now.
Those words I love you
Echo in my head,
The laughs and the smile that would follow.
I wish so badly
I didn't put up those walls
Because maybe then,
You could have seen the real me.
I know you would be proud,
They tell me you're proud and
That you're always watching,
But I can't help that a part of me
Hates the way I was back then.
I ache for a relationship with you,
A hug from you,
An encouraging message.
But now all I have
Are those one sided I love you's
And the feelings of those awkward hugs.
The way your arms would welcome us,
Wide open with a smile.
I can't help but cry
Because I can't even remember
The last time I hugged you.
I hope you always knew
How much I loved you,
How much I do love you.

Meeting you was like a breath of fresh air at a time that I
was drowning.
You came to me unexpectedly
Taking the water out of my lungs,
Allowing me to breathe again.
Although you had frayed edges and dangerous ways,
You intrigued me like no other.
You were broken too
But I was there for you in times of need.
You engulfed me in your words and held me close by
But in the end,
I was just another cigarette to you.
You threw me away with ease
And lit up the next one.

I found a girl worth writing about
But in the end I was left with nothing but words
Strewn across pages and pages of my journal;
A permanent ink to always remember
The way she made me feel
When I looked her into her eyes
And saw forever.

I was as fragile as paper
Yet you were fiery matches,
Striking me up and burning me down
Consuming me with toxic black smoke,
Suffocating me whole.

The waves crashed over my head
While I was drowning below.
Choking on the water that started to fill my lungs,
Suffocating beneath the power of the vicious storm
submerging me.
I'm drowning in my own emotions
And I'm gripping at whatever I can
To get back to shore.

I wonder what my life would be like
If I was able to formulate the feelings I have
Residing in the back of my brain.
Unable to get out,
Because I was never allowed to express myself.
Because showing my feelings
Meant discomfort for those around.
I wonder what my life would be like
If I was offered the openness to be free
To express
And to feel.

I'm only 21
Yet I've been to more funerals
Than I have dinner parties
And what a sad reality that is.

When I first met you
I imagined there would be more to our story.
More than the time I spent loving you and calling you
mine,
More than the goodbyes you sent
When you decided that our story
Wasn't what you wanted.
It's funny when I look at it now
Because growing up I was always told
I had such an intense sense of imagination.
That I had to tone it down because
*"what you imagine won't always come true."*
Yet here I am all this time later,
Torn apart
And trying to put the pieces together.
All because I let my imagination get the best of me
After crafting a picture perfect love story,
That I wished so badly would come true.

They tell me I'm a blend made perfectly
Of both my mother and father,
Yet I've never been able to pinpoint exactly what traits
they mean.
Is it my mother's round nose and caring personality,
Or my father's baby blue eyes and curly blonde hair?
Is it my mother's anxiety and passiveness,
Or my father's anger and temper
Causing him to blow his fuse at the smallest
inconvenience?
They say the good outweighs the bad
But I look at myself and all I see
Are the traits I would never want to pass onto my children.
The faults in my parents that have leaked into me.
So tell me,
Is that blend really so perfect?

My mind has become distant
And the empty body that remains feels nothing like my
own.
It's as if I'm just a lost soul
Wandering through crowded places,
Simply just existing in a place where I don't belong.
Every so often
I feel these little glimmers of peace
And realness that ground me.
But it's not long before my head becomes a fog
And I'm coasting through the day,
Left bewildered and confused
In a place that doesn't seem real anymore.

*- ghost in my own body.*

When they tell you to never make a home out of a person,
Please listen.
Because when she walked into my life
And wrapped me in her arms,
I was overwhelmed with this immense feeling of security -
Of home.
Yet now she's gone and all that is left
Are broken walls
And shattered windows
And I'm not quite sure
Where to go from here.

From the start
The love I had for you was full like the sun,
Glowing and radiating onto you.
But I think your love for me
Was more like the moon.
It came in phases
And what once started out as full,
Slowly but surely
Came to an end.
All that was left was a sliver,
Which eventually became darkness.
And just like the moon,
It would one day go back to being full
But you just couldn't bear
To wait around for that.

You keep showing up in my dreams
And I'm trying so hard to interpret what it means.
I feel like it has always been a guessing game with you.
The way you withdrew countless times,
Leaving me wondering what happened.
Or the way you left so abruptly
Without even giving me the chance.
You left me guessing what I did wrong,
What I could do to fix it
And what you meant when you said you loved me.
And somehow,
Months down the road,
When I finally think the games are done,
My brain has an evil way
Of bringing you back into view.

The trees were full and blossoming
Just like the love we had for each other.
You brought beauty to my life after a cold and grey winter,
But not long after,
Once the trees started changing
And the autumn leaves fell off,
So did our love.
Our love slowly changed with the seasons
And as beautiful as that sounds,
Once again
The winter approached and brought with it
The oh so familiar
Grey and gloomy clouds surrounding me.

In between the smiles and kisses,
There were unrequited I love you's and broken promises.
There was talk of a future that could never be built upon
Because the two engineers designing it
Were never meant to work together.

I just want to know if you know,
Are you watching?
Do you see the way my smile beams?
The way I flow through life,
So magically and full,
So comfortable in my skin.
Do you see the way I don't shy away
When someone asks me about my love life?
Do you hear me when I talk to you?
When I cried tears of happiness at my first "out" pride,
And sadness
Knowing you never got to experience it with me.
Your words of support echo in my mind
And even though you never got to know this version of
me -
The happy, comfortable, confident one -
I wouldn't be me
Without your words of support.
You knew exactly what I needed
When I didn't even know myself.

Grief is funny because
Now I'm left to remember you
For longer than I have known you in the physical world.
I still have a whole life ahead of me while you're stuck
frozen in time
In the minds of those who love you.
All we have left are the memories and moments,
The what if's and why's
Locked away in a small part of our mind,
Brought back up at the most random of times.
You think you're doing better and finally past the grief
stages,
But it pops back up.
That's the one thing they don't seem to tell you about
grief…
It's a lifelong process that never ends.
You will never stop missing the ones that you love,
You will never stop wishing they were back in your
presence,
And you will never stop holding love for them in your
heart.
All you can do is take those moments and see them as
gifts -
Gifts in the form of memories and pain,
Happiness and sadness,
From those you loved most.
So although they may not be with us in the physical world,
Please know they are still well and alive
With those precious, precious gifts.

And what do you do
When you never planned on living this long?
I've made it this far
But never did I think I would
*Actually make it this far.*
How am I supposed to exist
In a time that I never planned for?

He is the man
Who is supposed to teach.
He taught me a lot of things;
How to cook,
The rules of our favourite sport,
How words can hurt,
How to walk on eggshells.
I can't help but think of him
When sautéing onions.
The way the flavours
Bring tears to my eyes
Just like his words did.
He taught me many things
And I'm trying my best
To learn how to outweigh
The good
From the bad.

It's hard to explain to someone who wouldn't understand.
Those mornings that you wake up and already feel like
you've ran a marathon but came in last place,
The feeling of heaviness and exhaustion weighing on you,
The sense of being buried alive so deep that you never
have a chance of escaping.
It's hard to tell someone that you're not going to be able to
participate in the day when you don't even have a reason
as to why.
That's the thing about depression,
It overcomes you out of nowhere with no explanations or
why's.
You suddenly just feel defeated and exasperated at the
mere thought of putting your feet on the ground and
climbing out of the comfort and safety of your bed.
So, the next time someone tells you that they've already
failed for the day,
Please don't pry for a why.
Because sometimes,
The simple understanding of our lack thereof going on in
our mind,
Allows us to be okay.

There are many times that I get jealous
Of the way other people live their life so "normally."
But then I remind myself that upstairs in my brain
Is like an endless maze,
With chemicals rerouting themselves,
Getting lost,
Misinterpreting the natural communication that is
supposed to happen
And ultimately leading to a dead end.
It's like
Being so sure of the destination at hand,
But still not being able to provide the means necessary
To arrive at point B.
I get jealous of the fact that
These stupid pills are what allow me to function
At almost a "normal" level with society.
My doctor said they would allow my brain to produce the
needed chemicals
To help me succeed in everyday life,
Yet all they've done is leave me empty and reliant on
directions,
When I wish so badly, I could get to point B confidently.
Like a tour guide on a road trip,
Knowing just what needs to be done to get there.
Like everybody else
Whose brains are organized maps,
With a steady flow of traffic
Free of jams and chaos.

They say that when you exist and survive in chaos for so
long,
You don't know how to live in peace.
For the longest time I never understood what they meant
when they said that.
Until my therapist asked how I was doing
And I couldn't find the words to say that I was actually
doing
*Okay.*
She says it seems like I'm always searching
For something chaotic to be happening in my life.
I realized then
That existing in a world full of chaos and anger
Since the minute I was born,
Has shaped me into a human who thrives within the
chaos.
And without it
I don't quite know
How to accept
That I'm okay.

Grief isn't something that goes away with time.
The feelings might become less
And you might not let it overcome you completely
But it will always exist,
You just learn to grow around it.
Grief comes with me to every new connection I make,
Every conversation about family and loss
Which seems to be inevitable when meeting new people.
I encounter it again
When I pause to think about the person I was
And the person I will be -
How the person I will be,
Will never be a person *with* them.
I have been left to figure out how to live a life without
those I love,
All I know is I'm trying best to make sense of it all.

Safety.
People always say how important it is to find those safe
people in your life,
The ones who break down the walls and see you for you.
The ones who see your scars and only try to understand
your pain.
The ones who wrap you in warmth as you become
vulnerable and emotional.
You tell them that every time you let someone in behind
your walls,
You end up feeling less than safe in the end.
They always say the same thing though,
*That they don't want to hurt you,*
*That they won't hurt you.*
So, you let them in.
But surely with time,
Those feelings you promised to never allow yourself to
feel again
Always come back.
And just like last time,
You're left to pick up the pieces of the broken down walls
All on your own.
You build them back up but each time you do,
They're always a little bit stronger than last time.
Because the only time you've ever felt safe,
Was by yourself
With the comfort of those familiar walls protecting you.

There was a time when all I wanted
Was to know you front to back,
Memorize each and every part of you in my mind.
But now I'm at a war with myself
While I try to forget
Every last remnant of you.

I really like to think that what we had was real,
That's what I tell myself at least.
It was the feeling of floating on cloud 9,
It was dreamlike, really.
But then I stop and remind myself,
Cloud 9 isn't real
And maybe
What we had
Wasn't either.

I miss you
Every spring
When the lilacs finally bloom.
Every summer
When the fields fill with wildflowers and the sky is golden.
Every fall
When I'm walking through the crunchy leaves, reminiscing
on how it was your favourite activity.
And every winter
When the smell of Christmas cookies is in the air.
I miss you then,
I miss you now,
And I think I'll continue to miss you
*Forever.*

Although I may have forgiven,
The little girl
Who wished for nothing but love and comfort
From the one who was meant to protect,
Will never be able to forget.

I've always been told that my heart is so big
And I love so hard.
I found that to be true
Because
When it came to loving you
I poured
And poured
And po
      u
       r
       e
        d.
Until there was nothing left to give anymore.
Until my heart had been poured dry of all the
Love inside of it.
I always find myself pouring into an empty cup though,
One that never seems to fill up,
A cup that never has any love to spare some extra.
So, I find what's left remaining
In the deepest crevices of me
And for some reason
I still choose to give it to you.

To my younger self:
I'm sorry.
I'm sorry that you picked up your fear of abandonment at such an early age.
I'm sorry that the man you were supposed to look up to and learn from showed you anything but safety on most days.
I'm sorry that all you ever craved was an adult to protect you in the scariest moments.
I'm sorry that so often you had to console yourself - because how dare you burden them with your feelings.
I'm sorry that you were just a little kid but so often you had to be the one stepping up to the plate at explosive times to become a peacekeeper.
I'm sorry.
I'm sorry that you never had the chance to be a kid.
I see you, and I love you.
I promise you that each and every day
I'll continue to heal you.

I am trying so hard to
Let love in.
But how can I do that
When the people who were supposed to teach me how to
love,
Who were supposed to show me healthy love
Did anything but?
How can I let love in
When they were never shown
How to love and be loved?
The generations of hurt
And misfortune
Leaking down the family tree
Like a poisonous sap,
Infecting each branch.
How can I let love in
While trying to stop the leak all by myself?

No matter how far away I get,
They somehow still
Have this venomous hold on me.
Their words and
Their actions,
The memories and
The pain,
Playing in the back of my head like
A horror movie.
Except this one is real life
And they're the villains.
Latching onto those they "love"
With poisonous teeth,
Inflicting pain and
Suffocating us.
Like a constant loop stuck on repeat
In the back of my mind.
Like a horror movie you can't turn off.

Missing you is like
Watching the tide reach for the shore,
But the tide is always low
And it never hits the shore.
And just like the shoreline,
You'll always be out of reach.
I'll never be able to see you again
And I'll miss you forever.

Sometimes I can't help but wonder
If you remember that night.
Was my body language not strong enough
To show you I wasn't into you?
Was the way I pulled away from you mid kiss
Not enough to tell you?
Were the words *"no, it's okay, not right now"*
Spilling from my mouth
Not enough to convince you?
*Or maybe I didn't pull your hand away fast enough.*
*Maybe I could have been more upfront.*
*Maybe I gave you the wrong idea.*
Maybe when another four years pass,
I'll finally be over it.
Maybe you'll never remember,
Maybe that's what eats me alive.

> *- do you even know what you did?*

Your actions and words
May be different these days,
But the hurt child in me
Will never forget.

I wish I could go back in time,
Hold my nanny in my arms
And the moms that came before her,
And tell them,
You do not need a man to make you whole.
You do not need to settle when
You should be pursuing your dreams.
I wish I could show them
What true love is,
What it means to be loved unconditionally.
And maybe then,
My mom would never have settled,
Never have gone back to what hurt her most.
And even if that means I wouldn't be here
At least she would know what true love
Really is.

finding the light

To My Future Self,

Love yourself. Be honest with yourself. Belong to yourself
fully.
Acknowledge what you want and all your desires. Accept
every opportunity that comes your way. Learn when to
walk away and when to put your whole heart into it.
It's impossible to never *not* get hurt in life but remember...
you will always be able to break through the clouds that
are blocking you from the sunlight.
Stop giving your all to people who use you as their muse,
who see you as a temporary destination. You deserve
someone who loves you and never *stops* loving you.
You've made it this far. I'm proud of you.
Keep learning and never forget to live the life you love.

I hold so much resentment
Towards my past,
Constantly asking
*Why me?*
*Why didn't life just give me the upper hand?*
But I never stop to acknowledge
Past me.
The little version of me
Who carried me through all those years,
Who kept on keeping on
Even when they felt like they couldn't anymore.
The one who got me to where I am today.
And to that little version of me,
I promise that from here on out,
I'll offer compassion and warmth
And allow myself to heal.
Allow myself to grow through the bitterness
And become the person we always dreamed of.

Letting go
Is the
Start
Of finding
Myself
All over again.

I saw a post that said
*"Don't forget,*
*It's your parents first time*
*Experiencing life too."*
And I can't help but think of my dad
As a kid,
Who ached for the love and
Acceptance
Of his parents.
Who was seen as the black sheep
Because he refused to fit into
The boxes crafted for him and his siblings.
My dad who struggles
To show emotion and affection
And creating close bonds with his own kids.
My dad who probably never
Felt appreciation or praise
From the ones who made him.
There are so many times I wish
My dad was different during our childhood
But still,
I hold space for the hurt child inside him
And hope one day
He holds space for that inner child too.

I fell out of love with myself
When I started to fill the void within me
With one sided promises and hopeless love.
I drowned myself in alcohol
Hoping to feel anything but the emptiness
That leached through to my bones.
I fell into the toxic environment that gave me a temporary release
And was reminded in the morning as I woke with headaches
And the thought of my past heartaches,
That I can't fall in love with myself
While I'm filling other people's hearts for a sliver of time,
When I should be filling my own
Permanently.

She's a warrior.
She's the head of her herd,
Protecting those closest to her,
Never letting down or giving up.
She is a force to be reckoned with
Fiery and bold, one you can always count on.
She's been through hurricanes,
Earthquakes,
Natural disasters
Disrupting her life and bringing her down with the
damage.
But she always got back up.
She flew through all the ruckus around her,
Creating a beautiful masterpiece with her life.
She's a beautiful disaster.
She's my rock,
My best friend,
My older sister.

*- elizabeth.*

Do not come into my life
And treat me like a vacation,
A place for you to run to
And leave just as quick.
I am not your temporary getaway,
I am a home.
I am a mansion full of elegance and grace
And I refuse to be seen
As anything less than.

My coffee never needed the milk or sugar,
Just like I never needed you.
I had become so enthralled in the idea of having you,
Thought that you being by my side and in my mind
Made everything so much sweeter.
But I forgot who I was before you came along;
I was strong,
Powerful,
Bitter at times when needed.
I was not for everyone
And was only meant for those who were confident and
strong willed.
You added a new light to my life when you were mixed
into my darkness
Yet I still never needed you to make me whole.
The need for you was out of desire and lust,
The need for something tasteful and sweet in the moment.
But I am strong on my own,
I have become confident in who I am without the extra
additives,
The extra lust or love that romance brings.

I told myself I wouldn't do it,
Yet somehow, I found myself
In the same position again
Where I let down my walls
For an ill minded lover
Who had no intention to create a home.
How can someone hold your heart in their hands,
Fill it with so much colour and warmth
And allow it to feel something magical
Only to throw it right back on the ground once they've decided
It isn't for them anymore?
That heartbreak alone is enough
To make someone never want to get close again.
So I promise myself this;
I will not let these bricks down
Until someone has shown me the tools they have,
And the intricate blueprints they've constructed
To build a stable home.
A safe home,
That will never bring pain
To my heart again.

You can do this.
You can do whatever it is that your heart is yearning for.
This is your sign
To go for it.
Stop building that box around yourself,
Stop confining to the comfort
Of being hidden away
When you were meant to shine.
You are meant to do great things
And one day when you find that thing
That sets your whole soul on fire,
You'll be thankful
You stopped waiting.
Stopped confining,
Stopped blocking yourself off,
From the life that is yours.

*- the sign to do whatever you have dreamed of.*

Oh sweet friend,
I hope you know
That you deserve more than someone
Who is able to leave so easily,
When all you did
Was fight so hard
For them to stay.

*- you deserve a love that's confident*

Dear sweet darling,
I promise you this -
The light will shine,
And the sun will rise.
And when the clouds pass by,
And the rain finally stops,
You'll be thankful
That you kept going.
That you chose to see one more day.
    - *the sun will always rise again.*

To the women who stood before me,
Who fought for our legacy and our rights -
The ones who inspired future generations to come.
The ones who were dealt great sufferings and
The ones who stood resilient in the face of adversity.
Because of you I stand,
Because of you I have gained rights that were unspeakable
of in past years.
Because of you I will continue to fight.
Fight for future generations,
For greater equality for all us women,
For better futures for the young girls everywhere.
So they will never know what inequality against women is.
So they will rise.

Strong,
Resilient,
Powerful.
She's the skyscrapers withstanding earths powerful storms.
The feeling of warmth when the evening sun
Shines through your windows and drapes you in comfort.
She's the mother wolf,
A natural born protector
Ready to do whatever it takes for her family.
Her spirit is one that will bring anyone that natural feeling
Of acceptance and love.
She's got the beauty and grace everyone is drawn to.
Nurturing,
Wise,
Angelic
She's my mother.

*- and I dream to be half the woman she is one day.*

People who have never painted will throw the whole piece
away
When the paints have mixed together,
Creating a colour they weren't expecting.
But to artists and creators,
They can look at the colour made from a mistake
And turn it into a work of art.
So next time you look at yourself,
And see the bruises and rough edges,
The parts that so many others would quickly turn away
from...
Remember that you are the artist of your own life.
You have the power to create something spectacular and
mesmerizing,
Something everyone will want a glance of.
You will have a story to tell,
Just like the artist who saw beauty
In their mistakes.

Perhaps one of these days
I will pour the same love I give to everyone else,
Into the person that matters the most.
I'll fill myself with an abundance of love
And self care
And watch as I blossom like the lilacs each spring.
One of these days
I will learn to love myself.
So beautifully and intimately.

I want to fall in love with living.
I don't just mean living as in the act of getting by each day,
*No.*
I want to fall in love with being alive.
I want to fall in love with the way the sun sets and rises,
something beautiful and unique every day.
I want to fall in love with the nonsensical things of day to
day life;
Having a cup of coffee, eating a good meal, going for
walks, and getting out of bed.
I want to fall in love with being blessed with another day,
not feeling so heavy about what's to come and dreading
the unknown.
I want to fall in love with the chance to meet someone
new at any moment, strangers simply existing, who don't
even realize someone is falling in love with the idea of
them.
I want to fall in love with hearing new music, watching a
new show or reading a new book.
I want to fall in love with the way the leaves are falling as
the seasons change, because although one good thing is
ending there will always be a beautiful start for the next.
I want to fall in love with learning new things, trying
something I've never done before, experiencing something
I never thought I would.
I want to fall in love with myself, allowing myself to fully
experience life in a completely different mindset.
And until that day comes, whenever it is,
I'll teach myself to fall in love with the idea of it all.
The idea of being so carefree and full of hope
That maybe,
Tomorrow won't be so heavy.

I look at myself and can't help but see
The mess that I've become.
The layers upon layers of anxieties,
Stacked so high they've become unbearable.
The heart that is being held together by threads
After all the breaks and hardships life has brought on.
The childhood wounds begging to be loved on
And healed by the softest touch.
I wish so badly to love myself
And all the delicate intricacies that make up my existence
as a whole.
The way a mother sees a child's painting -
Messy,
With colours outside the lines,
And thinks
*What a lovely creation,*
*What a beautiful mess.*
     *- you are a beautiful mess that deserves love.*

Growing up in a home that feels as if it's on fire at most times, you slowly develop an eye for the slightest hints of danger. You analyze conversations and footsteps, learn tones and behaviours and are always on the lookout for the next gust of oxygen that is ready to fuel that flame brewing beneath the floorboards.

As you get older and move on from that fiery home, you hope to never be engulfed in those flames again - but that burned inner child inside of you will always be carrying that hyper alertness, fire-fighting tendency. Danger and fear are all that you know, so opening your eyes to safety and peace seems near impossible.

Allow yourself to feel safety.

Begin fighting those flames inside of you with peace and love.

Pour water onto that inner child and watch them grow through the burning fire.

Remind yourself each and every day that there is safety outside of the flames.

Let it be.
Remind yourself that
Not everyone will make time to listen to your thoughts
Or validate how you're feeling.
If someone is content with hurting you,
Then allow yourself to move past that.
Do not waste your time or your breath
On someone who is committed to shutting you down.
Remind yourself
You won't always receive closure.
Allow yourself to make peace with yourself,
Allow yourself to let go.

> *- wounds won't heal if you keep poking them.*

One day you'll wake up,
The sun will creep through your windows,
The air will feel a little lighter
And your mind will be a little clearer.
You won't feel so heavy.
And in that moment,
Everything is okay.

On days you tell yourself
It's not worth it,
Remember your inner child.
The one screaming for comfort.
The one who would have done anything in their power
To have someone like you,
To protect them in their most vulnerable times.
Think of your inner child,
Hold them close,
Give them a hug
And tell them
We will get through this.
    - *your inner child will thank you.*

It will hurt.
They're not lying when they say that.
And my god will it ever.
But please don't let those moments of discomfort
Stop you from becoming
The truest
And most loved version
Of yourself.
            - *healing.*

On the days that you feel a little lost,
A little less than,
Look up at the stars.
Remind yourself,
You're created with the same
Beautiful,
Captivating
Elements that fill the universe.
    *- your worth is forever infinite.*

For so long
My walls had been built up high.
High to ensure no one could get in,
To ensure I would never feel the same hurt I once did.
What a lonely life
I realized it was.
How can you live,
Guarded by the mere thought of feeling?
A fear built on believing that
Everyone will hurt me.
I kept myself lonely for so long
That I never realized it was only hurting me.
I hid myself away from those offering love,
Because how could anyone love
Someone so damaged,
Someone so scared?
Humans aren't meant to be lonely.
We are meant to be surrounded
By love
And happiness.
So I brought those walls down,
Slowly and surely
And realized
Just how beautiful
Life really is.
How fulfilling it is to be loved,
How exhilarating it is
*To live.*

Lessons for my past self:
You don't have to carry it all, you're allowed to ask for help.
Sometimes the people who let you down the most, are the ones who are supposed to love you forever.
Stop hiding yourself, you're missing out on so much joy and happiness.
Please don't allow yourself to believe that the hurt done to you is your fault, it's not.
Not everyone is meant for your love, your heart is huge and should only be given out to those who really deserve it.
You don't have to have it all figured out, what's meant to happen will happen in time.
If someone is showing you they aren't the one, please don't waste yourself away trying to see otherwise.
Stop dulling yourself down for the comfort of everyone else. Embrace your weirdness and quirks and all the silly things that make you unique.
It is okay to love even the darkest parts of yourself. And when you do, the healing and growth that will come with it will be unimaginable.
Just be you.
Forget about what everyone else has to say.

I'm sorry that you were never shown safety,
I'm sorry that you had to walk on eggshells
When you should have been jumping for joy
At the mere thought of being a kid.
    - *to my siblings and I.*

Every winter
The darkness consumes me
Like a black stormy cloud
Hovering above.
I tell myself the darkness finally won
But with every day that gets longer
And the seasons change,
I'm reminded…
Growth and light are coming
And Mother Nature never fails to prove this to us.
The gloominess
And cloudiness will finally let up
And you will see light.
You will grow from the darkness
And sprout with time
Just like the spring flowers
That withstood the dark, cold winter.

When you showed me nothing but fear,
That love was only ever conditional,
How dare you get angry
When I choose to love myself.
When I choose to protect myself,
When you never could.

    *- I'm no longer living inside your box.*

Despite
What you've been shown,
I promise,
You will never have to
Dull yourself down
For someone who truly loves you.

Dear sweet darling,
I promise you
Everything will be okay.
You are enough,
You have *always*
Been enough.
Please don't become someone you aren't
For someone who can't see
How worthy you are.
Please never lose sight of your true self.
Your sun will rise
And you will shine with time.

I look in the mirror
And see the
Tiny version of me,
The one who hurt and
Hid themselves away,
The one who thought
It would never get easier.
But oh sweet baby,
Just you wait.
The days will become lighter
And easier to carry,
I promise you this.
I'm so proud of you,
Look how far you've come.
I know how hard you fought
And I'm so proud
You chose to stay.
I'm living for you.

I remember being 16,
Looking at the pieces of me
That I thought were so broken
And never capable of being
Put back together into a
Mosaic of artwork.
Yet now 10 years later
I'm 26
And with time,
I've glued those pieces
Back together.
Reminding myself that
Pain is temporary
And what was once broken,
Can one day
Become a work of art.

finding love

*for michaela*

thank you for showing me what healthy love feels like.

I want to know your favourite flower and your favourite
season. I want to know about your family and all about
your childhood. I want to know your favourite colour and
your favourite movie, your favourite music, and your
favourite food. I want to know what keeps you up at night
and what makes you angry. I want to know what makes
you the happiest and what you love to do. I want to know
your dreams and desires, your goals and aspirations. I want
to know what made you, you.
I want to know you.

When I was little
I used to go to the field
And look up at the stars on hot summer nights.
When I met them,
A feeling of nostalgia rushed throughout me.
Their smile reminds me of a warm summer night,
Embracing you in its entirety
And keeps you longing for more.
And their eyes remind me of the shooting stars,
Mesmerizing and wishing for a forever.
Their touch is like the cool breeze,
A feeling of comfort on a hot night.
Being in their presence makes me feel calm
And it's as if I'm under that same night sky again
Looking up at the stars.
Yet this time I'm not looking at the stars in the sky
But the shining star
Curled up next me.

My head has always been a messy place,
A place that never knew comfort.
When I first met them though,
Everything in my mind went quiet.
They brought calmness to the hurricane
Building up inside me,
Calming my darkest storms and
Bringing light to my dark and gloomy life.
They are my sunshine on a rainy day.
They fill my life with happiness
And allow me to see through the clouds.
I became so used to the dark, stormy days
But ever since I met them,
I pray to god
My sunshine never goes away.

As long as I can remember as a kid I loved puzzles. I loved the time and problem solving it took to put all the pieces together and create such a beautiful piece of art. I'd glue the puzzle onto cardboard so I could keep it forever. Taking something that was so full of pieces, so messy and all over the place, and putting it back together as one was so riveting to me. As I got older I stopped putting puzzles together, I couldn't find the time and didn't have the patience to find all the pieces. But then I met you... I met you and suddenly there was nothing I wanted more than to take all your pieces and build them back up. I would spend hours trying to figure you out. To find out who you are. You're my lovely mess.
That missing piece I've been looking for, for so long.

Her eyes shine like warm morning sun,
Creeping through the cracks in your blinds
Slowly lighting up your whole room.
Her smile beams like a lighthouse at night,
Guiding the lost sailors back home through treacherous
storms.
Her voice is filled with softness and love,
It's the kind of voice that you want to record
And listen to forever.
Suddenly the brown in her eyes
Became my favourite colour,
I began searching for it everywhere I went.
Her smile was now my favourite view,
She guided me home with that smile
Through the disastrous mess of my mind
And the coldness of my heart.
Slowly but surely,
Everything about her became my favourite.

The walls were built sturdy and high,
Freshly completed with no chance of bringing them down.
Yet you came along and bit by bit
You took the bricks down,
Making your way to the fragile heart that sat within.
You held it in your hands
And felt the coldness
Of the past one sided lovers and broken promises.
Your touch was warm
And embraced it completely,
Allowing it to feel something
That was truly remarkable,
Something that was so different than the others.
With the promises that you won't be like everyone else,
The bricks have been put away,
In hopes they'll never have to be constructed
Into a prison like wall
So no ill minded lover
Can break through again.

I've never been one
That liked the idea of "meant to be,"
It was always something
That didn't seem attainable to me.
How could there be only one person in the world
Who fit you like a puzzle piece?
Yet when I'm next to you
And in your arms
Curled up so perfectly together,
I realize that nothing has ever felt so right.
You are my missing puzzle piece,
And nothing will ever compare.

Home.
Something I've never known before,
Something that has never wrapped me in comfort or
peace.
But then you came along
And showed me how true the phrase is,
*"That sometimes*
*Home is not always four walls, but a person.*
*How home isn't a place, but a feeling."*
You bring me that unfamiliar feeling
Of tranquility and warmth,
You've made me feel safe in your arms,
So loved and complete.
The flames that ignite inside of me
When I think of my childhood home
Are extinguished
When you wrap your arms around me
And hold me tight.

      *- you are my home.*

The world is crashing down around me
Yet all I can think about are their beautiful eyes
And loving energy.
I should be in a state of panic,
Yet somehow having them near
Brings me complete
*Serenity.*

That smile shined at me like a lighthouse at night,
Guiding the lost sailors back home.
She guided me home and into her arms,
And I've never felt more at peace before.

They trace their fingers across my skin while I fall asleep,
And I'm suddenly reminded
What it feels like
To be wanted.
*- they started a fire within me and I never want it to go out.*

I have become mesmerized by this work of art that sits in front of me,
The uniqueness and beauty she exhibits is truly breath taking.
I want to learn every inch of her like the back of my hand,
Engrave her in my memory
And never lose sight of the beauty that she is.
All I can think about is her.
She is my favourite work of art
And I'll never stop admiring her.

The house is made up of fragile beams and uneven bricks,
Placed together in ways that aren't completely stable
But have withheld the weathered storms.
There's creaky doors and cracked windows,
Flimsy and worn floor boards
And a dilapidated roof that could use some tlc.
Everyone that looked at the house tossed around the idea
of investing in it,
Making it their home - yet no one thought it was
worthwhile.
But when you walked in, you saw the potential.
You saw what it could be
And the beauty that could be created with some love and
care.
I am that house.
And for so long I struggled and fell apart
No one willing to stick around to see what could be
created from the mess.
Yet with you it's been different;
You dived into my life and invested your time,
Showed me love and care in all its forms.
And with you
I have become a home.

It's the soft kisses in the morning
As we wake intertwined amongst each other
In the warmth of the night before
A feeling so safe and refreshing.
   - *I wish these moments were infinite.*

You're summer
And I'm winter
You shine with warmth
And I'm filled with cold bitterness
But on those days that we are together
You are the bright sun glistening
Bringing warmth and light
To my once dark life.

Please don't settle. Find the person who loves you at your worst. The person who will learn you and love you and all the dark sides of you. Find someone who will accept you on your bad days and offer your comfort when you need it most. The person who will remind you to eat and makes sure your favourite safe foods are always available. Find the person that offers to do a little extra on the days you can't seem to find the energy to pull your weight. The person who remembers your favourite things and gets you small gifts that remind them of you - just so they can see you smile.

And on those days that you think that person doesn't exist, please be patient. I promise you there is someone out there. Someone who is safe and warm and full of love and acceptance.

And when you find that person, please never let go.

I know it's you.
I've known since
The moment
You wrapped me
In your arms.
I've never known
Peacefulness
Until then.

Growing up in a home that felt as if it was always on fire,
I never knew what it was like to feel secure with someone
else.
Until I stumbled upon you.
You made me feel warmth,
But not the type caused by the burning flames of my
childhood home.
You showed me warmth with your heart
And allowed me to be safe
And the feeling I was searching for
For so long,
Was now right in front of me.
*- this is the safety I've always craved.*

People never really cared to know me for the most part.
They always saw me as a short term fling
In between the ones that matter,
Like a commercial that people skip through
Just to get to the movie.
No one ever cared to see me, for me,
In all that I am.
It's different with you though
You look at me like I'm someone.
Someone to know,
Someone to learn,
Someone to love,
Someone to keep.
You looked at me
*And I've never stopped feeling seen since.*

I've tried to put into words
The love I have for you
But I never know how to explain
Just how magical it is.
It spans wider than the Great Plains,
And is deeper than all the seven seas combined.
It's more enlightening than space as a whole,
And as captivating as the midnight sky as it shines with the
northern lights.
It seems silly to compare our love to such beautiful things
When only the space between us
When our hearts connect
Knows exactly what our love is.
Because nothing is more beautiful
Than the love that is ours.

I'm surrounded by art of world renowned artists,
Pieces of work that are truly priceless.
Yet nothing is more mesmerizing
Than the masterpiece beside me.
    *- thoughts while at the art institute of chicago.*

I never knew what it meant to feel real love,
Until I met you.
I never knew what it felt like
To give my heart to someone
And feel safe.
Love has always been a foreign thing for me.
Yet you've opened my eyes to just how colourful
And beautiful love really is,
You've given me a safe place to rest my heart
And I hope it can stay here forever.

I've hurt
And broken into pieces.
My walls have been torn apart
And put together clumsily
To prepare for the next ill minded lover that comes my
way.
I thought I would never feel safe
To let someone in
And see behind those walls.
But you sat there patiently,
Set each brick aside
Piece by piece,
Softly and gently,
Until you reached my guarded heart.
And from that moment on,
You've held it with love and warmth
And proven to me every day,
Healthy love does exist.
You've proven to me without failure that
*Love is worth it.*

I've never been a morning person,
But when the sun creeps through the window
And I feel your body next to mine,
You look up at me and smile
*"Good morning baby."*
Suddenly,
My mornings have become more peaceful
And my days even brighter.
I find myself looking forward to these moments
And every morning to come
If it means waking up
Next to you.

If anyone asked me about love,
I'd tell them about you.
I'd tell them how it feels to be nurtured
And cared for
Without condition.
I'd tell them how you look at me with sparkling eyes,
A constant smile on your face,
And the overwhelming sense of certainty.
I'd tell them how love can be safe,
And warm,
And easy.
I'd tell them that love is worth it.
That there's nothing more beautiful than letting love in.

Over and over,
I was falling
Into the arms
Of those who refused
To hold on -
Until I met you.
You caught me and
Never let me go,
Held me tightly in your arms,
Ensuring I never
Fall again.

For so long
I've been craving a home.
I'd scour for what felt like centuries
To try and find one that felt
*Just right.*
But how could I have known
Until I met you,
That home would come in the form of
Two arms that wrap me in warmth,
A smile that glows through the night
And words that flow like honey.
How could I have known that home
*Could feel like this?*

Being indecisive
Has always been one of my worst traits.
Maybe that's why I surprised even myself
When I never thought twice
About you.
> - *you are the one.*

A list of things I'm falling in love with in 2023:
The morning sun coming through the bedroom window,
Cold morning walks to the coffee shop,
Almond milk mochas,
*You.*
The way my natural curls look,
Red light kisses,
Making playlists,
*You.*
Filling my body with good food,
The way my mind is forever expanding,
The simple things in life,
Experiencing so many firsts,
*You.*

     *- I think I love you.*

Rejection has always been my biggest fear
*But I think I love you.*
Maybe that's why telling you
Felt like jumping off a cliff that never seemed to end.
*Just tell them.*
What if you don't say it back?
*Just tell them.*
You asked me what was on my mind,
Why can't I say it?
*Just fucking say it.*
"I think I love you."
*I don't think, I do.*
*I love you more than I thought was possible.*
*Maybe this will soften the blow.*
You laughed and got flustered,
*I knew I fucked up.*
"I think I love you too."
    *- the start of forever.*

"Do you ever feel like things align perfectly when you least
expect it?"
You asked me that on our first date,
You were talking about the random outdoor patio set
In the middle of the cafe,
That just so happened to be set up
In the midst of everyone else.
*Like it was meant for us.*
"Yeah, sometimes things just don't seem real,"
I responded.
But not about the random patio set,
*This* doesn't seem real.
Being here with you doesn't seem real.
But somehow the stars aligned,
Just like that patio set
And brought you to me.
And ever since then
Life hasn't felt real.

*- you are a dream.*

It's 2am,
You're sleeping next to me
And I'm racking my brain
Trying to figure out
How this is real.
Someone pinch me.
*This must be a dream.*
Life has never felt
So blissful before.
But I'm still awake,
And I hope this dream
Never ends.

The way you held me so gently,
Caressed my body with such tender hands,
No rushing or prying.
You allowed me to feel safety
At the hands of someone else.
   *- a feeling I've never experienced before.*

Your eyes remind me of;
The warm coffee I sip on a cold morning,
Sweet honey and caramel,
Endless forests with just enough sunlight.
Your eyes remind me of;
Everything I've always craved,
Everything I'd wish to get lost in.
> *- lost in you and I never wish to be found.*

You were the light
Cracking through the darkness within me.
You saw the parts of me
That I was scared to let out,
And you illuminated them with passion.
You shone on them
Like they were a
Sight to be seen,
Like they were *meant to be seen*.

I'm thankful for a love like ours
In a time that we can be free.
A love that isn't hidden away
Behind closed doors,
Or masqueraded as less than love.
A love that is comfort,
And safe,
And ethereal.
A love that inspires,
A love that defies history.
A love that is loud.
*A love that is ours.*

They tell me that our love is a sin
And if that means
Being in her bed,
Or holding her hand in public,
Then baby;
I'll never stop sinning.
Because the only thing hotter than hell
Is the warmth I feel next to her
As she is wrapped up in my arms.

They ask me,
"How do you know they're the one?"
I respond in the best way I know how,
"Because they brought out my inner child,
Held them so softly and gently
And never stopped loving them since."

Your kisses
Are as soft
As the poetry
I write for you.

## acknowledgements

thank you to Michaela for encouraging me to make my words available to the world and guiding me with love along the way. to Elizabeth, for always reading my poems at all hours of the night and offering advice and suggestions to better them, thank you for being such a wildly supportive older sister. to my parents, thank you for teaching me how to make the best out of tough circumstances and creating something for myself, and for always believing in every decision I make. to my best friends, thank you for sticking it out with me, for being my chosen family and the ones always there when I need. to my book obsessed auntie andrea, I can only imagine how proud you would be of me for being published, thank you for always watching from up above.
and to every follower on the internet who showed me I'm not alone, thank you. I wouldn't be here without any of you.

about the author


jess norris (she/they) is a queer writer from Canada who started sharing their thoughts from their notes app on tumblr around 2015. "your sun will rise again" is their first collection of poetry, with poems going all the way back to 2015. "your sun will rise again" is a collection of poems in three stages: into the darkness, finding the light and finding love. these stages showcase the healing journey jess has been on and how it led them to the light – finding a safe love. it is a collection of poetry for those who feel things deeply, for the ones learning how to find love within them and for those who have been hurt by others and the boxes that have been placed on them.
jess is passionate about healing and growth and watching those around them thrive. they hope that this collection of words touches the ones that happen to read them.

connect and follow along on their journey:
tiktok: @wordsby.jn
instagram: @wordsbyjn

Made in the USA
Monee, IL
11 February 2024

53326529R00083